KEVIN DURANT
Basketball Superstar

BY MATT DOEDEN

CAPSTONE PRESS
a capstone imprint

Sports Illustrated KIDS Superstar Athletes is published by Capstone Press,
1710 Roe Crest Drive, North Mankato, Minnesota 56003.
www.capstonepub.com

Books published by Capstone Press are manufactured with paper
containing at least 10 percent post-consumer waste.

Library of Congress Cataloging-in-Publication Data
Doeden, Matt.
  Kevin Durant : basketball superstar / by Matt Doeden.
    p. cm. — (Sports illustrated kids: superstar athletes)
  Includes bibliographical references and index.
  Summary: "Presents the athletic biography of Kevin Durant, including his career as a high school,
college, and professional basketball player"—Provided by publisher.
  ISBN 978-1-4296-7682-3 (library binding) ISBN 978-1-4296-8004-2 (paperback)
  1. Durant, Kevin, 1988—Juvenile literature. 2. Basketball players—United States—Biography—
Juvenile literature. 3. Oklahoma City Thunder (Basketball team)—Juvenile literature. I. Title.
II. Series.
  GV884.D868D64 2012
  796.323092—dc23
                                                                        2011034033

Editorial Credits
Angie Kaelberer, editor; Ted Williams, designer; Eric Gohl, media researcher;
    Laura Manthe, production specialist

Photo Credits
Sports Illustrated/David E. Klutho, 1, 2–3; John Biever, 13, 22 (top); John W. McDonough,
    cover (all), 1, 5, 6, 9, 15, 16, 18, 19, 21, 22 (middle & bottom), 23, 24; Robert Beck, 10

Design Elements
Shutterstock/chudo-yudo, designerpix, Fassver Anna, Fazakas Mihaly

Direct Quotations
Page 8, from August 10, 2010, Ball Don't Lie, A Yahoo Sports Blog, by Trey Kerby,
    www.sports.yahoo.com/nba/blog/ball_dont_lie
Page 17, from May 1, 2010, *Houston Chronicle* article, "Lakers outlast Thunder," by Jonathan
    Feigen, www.chron.com.

Printed in the United States of America in North Mankato, Minnesota.
102011   006405CGS12

TABLE OF CONTENTS

CHAPTER 1

BRINGING THE THUNDER

All eyes were on **forward** Kevin Durant. He and the Oklahoma City Thunder needed to beat the Memphis Grizzlies to advance in the 2011 playoffs. Durant was one of the National Basketball Association's (NBA's) biggest stars. But in the previous game, he'd made only three of 14 shots.

forward—a tall, strong player who usually plays close to the basket

By the end of the first quarter, the Thunder were trailing. Durant had made just two of nine shots. Then he looked into the stands and saw his mother.

From that moment, Durant was unstoppable. By the end of the game, he had 39 points. The Thunder won 105-90. The team was on its way to the Western Conference Finals.

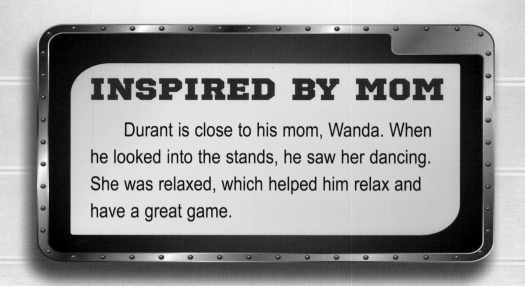

INSPIRED BY MOM

Durant is close to his mom, Wanda. When he looked into the stands, he saw her dancing. She was relaxed, which helped him relax and have a great game.

CHAPTER 2

EARLY SUCCESS

Kevin Wayne Durant was born September 29, 1988, in Washington, D.C. His mother, Wanda, raised him and his older brother, Tony. Even at a young age, Durant loved playing basketball. He tried to play like his favorite NBA player, Vince Carter.

"Playing outside is key for younger kids growing up. It builds that love for the game."
—Kevin Durant

Durant joined an **Amateur** Athletic Union (AAU) youth team called the Prince George Jaguars. At age 11, Durant led his AAU team to the national championship.

Durant became one of the nation's best high school players. As a senior, he averaged 23.6 points per game. He played in the 2006 McDonald's All-Star game and was named co-Most Valuable Player (MVP).

amateur—someone who participates in a sport without being paid

Almost every major college basketball program wanted Durant. He chose the University of Texas.

Durant was an instant star. He averaged 25.8 points and 11.1 **rebounds** per game during the 2006–2007 season. Texas went 25–10 and made the NCAA Men's Basketball Tournament. But the team lost to the University of Southern California in the second round.

rebound—the act of getting the ball after a missed shot

CHAPTER 3

NBA STAR

After one year at Texas, Durant decided to go to the NBA. The Seattle SuperSonics chose him with the second overall pick in the 2007 NBA **Draft**. In his first NBA game, he scored 18 points.

As a **rookie**, Durant averaged 20.3 points per game. He was named the league's Rookie of the Year.

draft—the process of choosing a person to join a sports team
rookie—a first-year player

In 2008 the SuperSonics moved to Oklahoma City and became the Thunder. The team didn't win many games. But Durant was getting better and better.

In the 2009–2010 season Durant led the NBA with a 30.1-point average. The Thunder reached the conference playoffs. They lost to the Los Angeles Lakers in the first round.

"People go through losses every year. But it's tough for us because we're so close. We definitely don't want to go home." —Kevin Durant

Durant and the Thunder were even better in 2010–2011. They went 55–27 and won the Northwest Division. They breezed past the Denver Nuggets in the first round of the playoffs, four games to one.

Durant's big 41-point performance helped the Thunder beat the Grizzlies in the second round. But that was as far as they could go. They lost to the eventual NBA Champions, the Dallas Mavericks, in the Western Conference Finals.

CHAPTER 4

DOMINANT FORCE

Durant is an amazing all-around player. He can hit long-distance shots or drive to the basket. He's a skilled passer and rebounder. His quickness makes him an excellent defender. Many NBA experts believe he could become one of the game's all-time greats.

SPECIAL NUMBER

Durant wears jersey number 35 in honor of his AAU coach, Charles Craig. Craig was 35 years old when he died in 2005.

TIMELINE

1988—Kevin Durant is born on September 29 in Washington, D.C.

2000—At age 11, Durant leads his AAU team to the national title.

2006—Durant graduates high school and goes to the University of Texas.

2007—Durant leaves Texas after one year and is drafted by the NBA's Seattle SuperSonics.

2008—Durant wins the NBA's Rookie of the Year Award. The SuperSonics move to Oklahoma City and are renamed the Thunder.

2010—Durant becomes the NBA's youngest scoring champion and leads the Thunder to the playoffs.

2011—Durant again leads the NBA in scoring. The Thunder reach the Western Conference Finals.

GLOSSARY

amateur (AM-uh-chur)—someone who participates in a sport without being paid

draft (DRAFT)—the process of choosing a person to join a sports team

forward (FOR-wurd)—a tall, strong player who usually plays close to the basket

rebound (REE-bound)—the act of getting the ball after a missed shot

rookie (RUK-ee)—a first-year player

READ MORE

Frager, Ray. *Oklahoma City Thunder.* Inside the NBA. Edina, Minn.: Abdo Pub. Co., 2012.

Frisch, Aaron. *Oklahoma City Thunder.* Mankato, Minn.: Creative Education, 2012.

Ladewski, Paul. *Megastars 2010.* New York: Scholastic, 2010.

INTERNET SITES

FactHound offers a safe, fun way to find Internet sites related to this book. All of the sites on FactHound have been researched by our staff.

Here's all you do:

Visit *www.facthound.com*

Type in this code: 9781429676823

 Check out projects, games and lots more at
www.capstonekids.com

INDEX